War of the Worlds

War of the Worlds:
What about Peace?

Bruno Latour

Translated from the French by Charlotte Bigg
Edited by John Tresch

PRICKLY PARADIGM PRESS
CHICAGO

Prickly Paradigm Press, LLC
5629 South University Avenue
Chicago, Il 60637

www.prickly-paradigm.com

ISBN : 0-9717575-1-8
LCCN : 2002 102649

Printed in the United States of America on acid-free
paper.

911

The lesson does not seem to sink in. When did Paul
Valéry prophetically observe that, "We have now
learned that all civilizations are mortal?" Just after
the so-called Great War. Many horrific disasters have
passed since, and yet we are still surprised when
another attack seems to threaten the precarious
forms of life so dear to our hearts. Since September
2001, we go on dialing the same emergency number,
911, and rightly so, since we have entered a state of
emergency. We look around frantically to understand
why all that we feel is worth fighting for remains so
fragile. I read in the news that Hollywood
scriptwriters rushed to revise the catastrophist

scenarios that suddenly looked obscene in the face of a much harsher reality. In the same way, nihilism used to look like a gold mine when it was applied hypothetically to any value worth its salt. Does such idle criticism not look superficial now that nihilism is truly striking at "us"—at US— putting what we call civilization in great danger of being found hollow? Who needs to add another deconstruction to a heap of broken debris? The courageous icono-clast waving her arm in defiance, so proud of her hammer, ready to break everything with the powerful weapon of critique—down with empires, beliefs, fetishes, ideologies, icons, idols!—does she not look a bit silly now that what she wanted to strike down lies in dust, already smashed to the ground, and by people who do not fit at all the ideal of the critical avant-garde?! What has happened to the critical urge? Has it not overshot its target?

The word "war" is spewing out of every mouth, and although it sounds so disheartening at first there might be an opportunity to seize on these clarion calls. In "emergency" lays a hidden word, "emer-gent." What is emerging, being "brought to light," by the recent events? To realize that we are in the midst of a war might take us out of the complacency with which so many people imagined an ever more peaceful future, with all the nations converging toward fuzzy modernist ideals. No, Westerners might not be able to modernize the whole planet after all. This does not mean that they are forever locked into the narrow confines of their own civilization, threatened by all others in a war of all against all. It just means that they counted a bit prematurely on possessing a sure principle that could unify the whole world, make one accepted common world. It is not the case that an already existing peaceful union has been savagely shattered. We have merely been reminded that unity has to be made; it is not simply observed. Far from being self evident, unity was never more solid than a future possibility to struggle for. Unity has to be the end result of a diplomatic effort; it can't be its uncontroversial starting point.

My argument in this tricky, prickly piece is that it might after all be better to be at war, and thus to be forced to think about the diplomatic work to be done, than to imagine that there is no war at all and keep talking endlessly about progress, modernity, development—without realizing the price that must be paid in reaching such lofty goals. So we are at war, aren't we? Fine. But then three questions can finally be raised: who is involved? What are their war aims? And finally, the most important one: what about peace? I will argue that we are not faced with a peace unfairly shattered, nor with a "war of civilizations," but that we have first to fathom that a war of the worlds has been raging all along, throughout the so-called "modern age"—this modern parenthesis. Still, nothing proves we are on the wrong side, and nothing proves either that this war cannot be won. What is sure is that it has to be waged explicitly and not covertly. The worst course would be to act as if there were no war at all, only the peaceful extension of Western natural Reason using its police forces to combat, contain, and convert the many Empires of Evil. That is the mistake those who still believe they are moderns are in danger of making. On the other hand, if we are going to bring the wars of modern-ization to an end, we cannot afford to declare that all bets are off, that premodern savagery will be met with premodern savagery, that senseless violence will answer senseless violence. No, what is needed is a new recognition of the old war we have been fighting all along—in order to bring about new kinds of negotiation, and a new kind of peace.

The false peace offered by the one nature/many cultures divide

If we are in a state of war, who are the parties engaged in this conflict? In earlier times things looked simpler: despite all their disagreements, their disputes and the diversity of their customs and languages, humans used to share, without even knowing it, a common world, the world of nature, that physical anthropology could describe fairly well. Thus the many diverse cultures known to social and cultural anthropology stood out against a back- ground of natural unity. They could be compared synoptically not unlike the way a museum's white

wall helps to bring out the differences between exotic
masks hung side by side. There may have been
Bantus and Baoules, Finns and Laplanders,
Californians and Burgundians, but they all shared a
common make-up of genes, neurons, muscles, skele-
tons, ecosystems and evolution which allowed them
to be classed in the same humanity. If cultural differences shined so vividly, this was because the unity of
nature provided the common denominator.

This denominator was even more indisputably
common when one moved from the world of human
nature to the world of non-human nature. The
possibility of disagreement among specialists or
disciplines certainly remained, but ultimately the
world (in the singular) external nature would be
enough to bring agreement among them all.
Different cultures existed, with their many idiosyncrasies, but at least there was only one nature with its
necessary laws. Conflicts between humans, no matter
how far they went, remained limited to the representations, ideas and images that diverse cultures could
have of a single biophysical nature. To be sure,
differences of opinion, disagreements and violent
conflicts remained, but they all had their source in
the subjectivity of the human mind without ever
engaging the world, its material reality, its cosmology
or its ontology, which by construction—no!
precisely, by nature—remained intangible.

In this blessed era of modernism, differences, in
other words, never cut very deep; they could never
be fundamental since they did not affect the world
itself. Agreement was in principle always possible, if
not easy. There always remained the hope that
differences of opinion, even violent conflicts, could
be eased or alleviated if one only focused a little
more on this unifying and pacifying nature and a
little less on the divergent, contradictory and subjective representations humans had of it. If, through
education, rational debates or careful scrutiny, one
succeeded in bringing the one natural and physical
reality into the debates, then passions would be
calmed. Thus one could always move from
passionate diversity to a reassuring and rational
agreed upon reality. Even if humanity featured divergent religions, rights, customs and arts, it could
always seek solace in this haven of unity and peace
offered by science, technology, economics and
democracy. Passions may divide us, but we can rely
on reason to reunite us. There may be many ways of
bringing up children, but there is only one embryo-
genesis. Therefore, when disputes occur, we need
only to increase the relative share of scientific objectivity, technical efficiency, economic profitability and
democratic debate, and the disputes will soon cease.

It is impossible now to realize the extent to which
this solution was convenient in solving the problem
of the progressive composition of the common world

(which is the name I give to politics). For after all, the hard work had already been done, unity had been fully constituted, fitted out from head to foot. The world had been unified, and there remained only the task of convincing a few last recalcitrant people who resisted modernization—and if this failed, well, the leftovers could always be stored among those "values" to be respected, such as cultural diversity, tradition, inner religious feelings, madness, etc. In other words, the leftovers could be gathered together in a museum or a reserve or a hospital and then be turned into more or less collective forms of subjectivity. Their conservation did not threaten the unity of nature since they would never be able to return to make a claim for their objectivity and request a place in the only real world under the only real sun. Like the wives and children of overthrown monarchs, who were locked up in convents for life, they would be forever banned from participating in the serious matters of state.

Anthropologists, curators, physicians, artists could even enjoy the luxury of "respecting" those diverse idiosyncrasies since they never threatened to stake a claim in the order of the world. There were certainly wars, innumerable ones, but there was only one world, which, without hesitation, made it possible to speak of one planet, one universal humanity, the rights of man and of human beings as such. In those not-so-distant times, there could have been no wars of the worlds. Diversity could be handled by tolerance—but of a very condescending sort since the many cultures were debarred from any ontological claim to participate in the controversial definition of the one world of nature. Although there could be many warring parties engaged in local conflicts, one thing was sure: there was only one arbiter, Nature, as known by Reason.

Of course, there remained a slight suspicion that the referee of all the disputes could be biased. Maybe this world in the singular, the world of Science, of Technology, of the Market, Democracy, Humanity, Human Rights—in short the world of the Human—suffered from being a little ethnocentric, if not a trifle imperialist, or even merely American, not to say Yankee…Unification proceeded, it was all too clear, in a somewhat unfair manner, as though the task of unifying the world had been delegated (although no one had actually delegated anything) to only one of the cultures of the world, the one bearing the imprecise name of the West. However odd, this in itself did not seem shocking to most Westerners and their many clients, because fundamentally "the West" was not a culture "among" others, since it enjoyed a privileged access to nature and its already-accomplished unification. Europeans, Americans, Australians and later Japanese certainly possessed cultural traits which identified them as unique cultural groups, but their access to nature

swiftly made these superficial differences disappear.
If "Westernization" could be challenged or rejected,
"modernization" was beyond doubt the common
property of humanity—and even if "modernization"
came to be disputed, then "naturalization" could
provide another, deeper uncontroversial bedrock
common to all.

Thus, surrendering to modernization and naturalization did not mean submitting to any given imperialism or voluntarily imitating a cultural model, but
rather coming closer to this fundamental, indisputable source of unification that was to be rooted in
a nature known by reason. The solution always was
to connect directly to the objective origin of the
common world and thus to draw nearer to unity.
Neither those who were developing nor those being
developed had the feeling that they were surrendering to another people when they respectively
disseminated or adopted sciences, technologies,
markets and democracy. They were surrendering to
modernization, which, because of its break with all
cultural inheritances, simply marked the more or less
dramatic eruption of nature, indisputable and
unifying—as if truth was finally shining through a
tear in the colorful screen clumsily painted by the
many cultural representations.

There was, however, a little hitch in this peaceful
modernist version of politics: nature was as meaning-

less as it was disenchanted! Herein lies the whole
paradox of these strange times we call "modernity"—
which retrospectively appear no longer as the motor
of history, but increasingly as the partial representation of one historical episode now come to an end.
For if nature had the immediate advantage of
imparting unification, it also had the serious draw-
back, in the eyes of its very promoters, of being
fundamentally devoid of meaning. Objective facts in
their harsh reality could neither be smelled, nor
tasted, nor could they provide any truly human signi-
fication. The modernists themselves were fully aware
of this, and even acknowledged it with a sort of sado-
masochistic joy. "The great scientific discoveries,"
they were glad to say with a shudder, "are incessantly
wrenching us from our little village and hurling us
into the frightening, infinite spaces of an icy cosmos
whose center we no longer occupy." Ultimately,
though, this was not a matter of choice: modernization compelled one to mourn the passing of all one's
colorful pretensions, one's motley cosmologies, of all
the many ways of life with their rich rituals. "Let us
wipe away our tears," the modernists liked to
declare, "let us become adults at last; humanity is
leaving behind its myth-imbued childhood and is
stepping into the harsh reality of Science,
Technology and the Market. It's a pity but that's the
way it is: you can either choose to cling to your
diverse cultures, and conflicts will not cease, or,
alternatively, you can accept unity and the sharing of

a common world, and then, naturally (in every sense of the word), this world will be devoid of meaning. Too bad, love it or leave it." One may wonder whether one of the many metaphysical origins of the twentieth-century world wars did not consist of this odd way with which the West sought to pacify all conflicts by appealing to a single common world. How long can one survive in peace when torn by this impossible double bind with which modernizers have trapped themselves together with those they have modernized: nature known by reason unifies, but this unification is devoid of meaning?

The irresistible advance of the modernization front had a great advantage, and that was to help define the difference between "us" and "them" as a great, radical break. The term "ethnocentrism" cannot by definition be applied to the West, contrary to what anti- and post-colonialists might claim, since the center was made of nature and not of any particular culture. Although ethnocentrism, like common sense according to Descartes, is of all things in the world the most evenly distributed, and although in establishing relations of trade, domination and avoidance, all peoples and all nations have placed themselves in the center, relegating the others to the periphery, the West, and only the West, was thought to have escaped this fate. Whereas all the others had maintained a fundamental equality between them, in that they were all at the very least peoples, as Lévi-

Strauss had often said, this was never the case for the modernists: the others were "peoples" and "cultures," but "we," the Westerners, were only "half" culture, as Roy Wagner has argued. For the first time in history, the West could occupy, alone, the position of undeniable center, without this center having a particular ethnic group as its origin. This was indeed precisely what enabled the difference to be established between "them"—prisoners inside the narrow confines of their cultures, incapable of grasping the unifying principles of nature—and "us," who evidently possessed more or less emphasized cultural traits, but whose hidden strength was to have reached, thanks to Science, Technology and Economics' slow work of erosion, the rock bottom of universality, the hard core of nature, the backdrop of any history. The modernizing West may have been "naturocentric" or "ratiocentric," but never had a political formation been less ethnocentric than it. All the more so, since with truly admirable magnanimity, it gave everybody, whatever his or her ethnic group of origin, the chance to become universal like itself. Through the mediation of scientific objectivity, technical efficiency and economic profitability, anybody could join this fatherland without ancestors, this ethnic group without rituals, this country without borders; this country of reason, able to access unifying nature through the hard work of criticism and rational discussion.

But in the end, the meaning of this existence still remained unsolved. For, the more one belonged to this fatherland without father or mother, the less this belonging had any significance: a strange paradox, which triggered a frantic search throughout the whole planet to discover the generic human being, who, when it was finally found, only led to despair at the sight of what had turned out to be again mere nature: animal, biophysical, genetic, neuronal—at best a sociobiological Darwinian machinery. The solution for diminishing, if not solving, this contradiction between a unifying but senseless nature, on the one hand, and, on the other, cultures packed with meaning but no longer entitled to rule objective reality, was to make the notion of "culture" sacred. Cultures began to be cherished, conserved, respected, reinvented, occasionally even made up from scratch.

But the notion of culture, it should not be forgotten, is relational: ethnic groups do not belong in the same ontological category as cabbages or turnips. Culture is but one of the possible ways of relating to others, one perspective on otherness, and certainly not the only one. Multiculturalism is nothing more than the flipside of what may be termed mononaturalism. The impression of great open-mindedness given by multiculturalism should not hide the price that peoples had to pay for the preservation of their existence in the form of culture. "You possess meaning, perhaps," they were told, "but you no longer have reality, or else you have it merely in the symbolic, subjective, collective, ideological form of mere representations of a world that escapes you, although *we are able to grasp it objectively*. And don't be mistaken, you have the right to cherish your culture, but all others likewise have this same right, and all cultures are valued by us equally." In this combination of respect and complete indifference, we may recognize the hypocritical condescension of cultural relativism so rightly criticized by Donna Haraway. To the eyes of the cultural relativist, those cultural differences make no real difference anyway, since, somewhere, nature continues to unify reality by means of laws that are indisputable and necessary, even if they are not as charming and meaningful as these delightful productions which human whim and arbitrary categories have engendered everywhere.

Let us sum up the situation as it was when modernization was at its height: a) we possessed a privileged, natural world already unified, whatever some humans imprisoned by their own symbolic representations might think; b) the West, alone in not being ethnocentric, contemplated the multiplicity of ways of evading this common world with a simultaneously watchful, dismayed, condescending, tolerant and interested eye; c) in addition, we could profit from the rich diversity provided by many cultures, all comparable, and all of them equally disengaged from the construction of the common natural reality, which was left safely in the hands of culture-free scientists, engineers, economists and democrats; d) as an added bonus, we were offered some sort of peace proposal which presupposed that there could be no conflict whatsoever, no real wars, no reality wars: worlds were never at stake, only the many symbolic representations of the one and only world; unity was already complete; a general increase in the dose of universal nature would bring agreement straight away. Finally, e) since this universal nature had no human meaning, cultural conservatism was indispensable for embellishing, enriching and ornamenting, by means of values and passions, the harsh world of facts and reason—provided, of course, that none of these cultures claimed any ontological pretensions. *Voila*, in a few words, the now vanished world which the alliance of mononaturalism and multiculturalism had proposed. "The one world is ours, the many worlds are yours; and if your disputes are too noisy, may the world of harsh reality come in to pacify your disputes." A peculiar offer of peace, one which had never recognized the existence of a war in the first place!

From mono- to multi-naturalism

Looking retrospectively at the episode of modernization—a few short centuries of violent spasms—one cannot help but be struck by the extent to which it was peaceful, despite the wars that were unleashed on an ever more staggering scale. This is not a paradox: the West was fundamentally peaceful since disagreements could never go very far. They affected representations, but they never touched the substance, the very fabric of the world. To speak like philosophers, only the "secondary qualities" were at stake, never the "primary qualities." To the Galileos, Newtons, Pasteurs, Curies, even to the Oppenheimers, politics always appeared—and still appears to Steven Weinberg—as a violent fire that a little more objective science could always snuff out. However terrifying the conflicts were, Westerners were all convinced that peace was always within arm's reach, just behind the narrow walls of our passions and our representations. How could they define any war aims? There was no war at all. Only the "others" were at war because of the archaic calling of their subjective passions.

Already we have forgotten just how reassuring, gratifying and stabilizing was this feeling of inner peace that the modernists enjoyed: this absolute certainty that there would be wars, but not wars of science; that there were wars in the world, but never wars of the worlds—except in science-fiction stories. For all those great ancestors, there existed no source of conflict that could not be wiped out. Or if it could not be made to disappear, it could always be internalized, psychologized, sunk into the private depth of our inner selves. This is what the West had managed so successfully with "religious peace." Yes, religion is divisive, but no, it does not involve the world, only one's private salvation. Religion had to become a mere culture so that nature could become a true religion—what brings everyone into assent. Living side by side implied no re-negotiation of the common world already constituted, but simply the acceptance of others' eccentricities, opinions and feelings—so long as they remained within the narrow boundaries of their cerebral movie theaters. What a perfect solution: the invention of a tolerant society.

But this solution is no longer available to those who no longer live under the sway of modernism. There are many ways to interpret modernism and its history, but I have become convinced that the best way is to treat "modernism" as an anachronistic interpretation of the events in which the West participated. In this sense the West has never been more modern than the French revolutionaries, in the eyes of Tocqueville and François Furet, have been revolutionary. Modernism has never been anything more than a highly biased interpretation of events with different and sometimes entirely opposite motivations. To be sure, modernism as a theory of what was happening has been active, and sometimes very efficiently, in molding the events, but it was never an accurate account of the strange ways in which the West became entangled with every nation and every living and non-living entity on Earth. How to reconcile, for instance, the war cry for emancipation, progress and detachment from any archaic constraint with the progressive imbroglios of humans and non-humans at an ever-expanding scale that characterizes the West? Which one of these three following phenomena should the anthropologist study most carefully: the self-congratulatory talk of the modernists about becoming at last released from the shackles of the past? The harsh reality of becoming more attached every day to ever more opaque hybrids of law, science, technology, passion and social ties? Or, should she follow instead the perverse ways through which the talk about progress interferes, accelerates, blinds and perturbs the many entanglements of humans and non-humans that are being generated on an ever-expanding scale? Whichever choice is made, there is no longer any overlap between modernism as an interpretation and the events it purported for so long to interpret. Through the cracks of the call for universal reason now appears a rather monstrous animal that no longer looks like "the West." If it has ceased to be familiar to the eyes of the anthropologist, it has lost also its inner peacefulness and, with it, its complete asymmetric distance from the "others." "They" look a lot like "us" now—and this is why we are finally at war with them, but what sort of battle are we expected to lead?

The slogan invented by journalists a few years ago has been well chosen: "Science Wars" are taking place. What looked at first like a tempest in a teacup has revealed itself as the tiny tell tale sign of a much larger transformation. One way to sum up this sea change is to say that modernity, which had been conceived as the filling up of the world with ever more matters of fact, is now full of what I would like to call states of affairs. Matters of fact were supposed to bring agreement by appealing to the objective nature out there; but instead many of the former facts have become controversial issues that create more dissent than agreements, thus requiring another quasi-legal or quasi-political procedure to bring closure. Facts are no longer the mouth-shutting alternative to politics, but what has to be stabilized instead. To use another etymology, "objects" which had been conceived as wholly exterior to the social and political realm, have become "things" again, that is, in the sense of the mixture of assemblies, issues, causes for concerns, data, law suits, controversies which the words *res*, *causa*, *chose*, *aitia*, *ding* have designated in all the European languages. While in earlier times, it was still possible to imagine quieting down the turbulent political passions by a solid importation of indisputable facts, the only possibility now seems to add to the turmoil of passions the turmoil generated by hotly disputed states of affairs. The fount of peace no longer exists "out there." In addition, cultures no longer wish to be mere cultures. We are now facing wars of the worlds. Mononaturalism has been replaced by a monster inconceivable only ten years ago: multinaturalism (to use the neologism devised by Eduardo Viveiros de Castro) which has joined in the devilish dance started by multiculturalism—after the latter was blown to pieces along with the hypocritical tolerance it entailed. No one wants to be just tolerated anymore. No one can bear to be just one culture "among others" watched with interest and indifference by the gaze of the naturalizers. Reality is once again becoming the issue at stake.

The conjunction of two words repeated ad nauseam, "globalization" and "fragmentation," constitutes a striking symptom of these changing times. It would be a mistake not to take these "globalloneys" very seriously, for they indicate, respectively, the crisis of unity and the crisis of multiplicity. Contrary to the misconceived impression that contemporary discourses on globalization might give, our age is much less global than it was, say, in 1790, 1848, 1918, 1945, 1968 or 1989, to take a few simple land-marks of particular significance to the Europeans. It was still possible at these different dates to speak of humanity, of the human being, of world unity, of planet Earth, of progress and of world citizens, since we were under the impression of having connected history to the single rational, learned, objective source of unity and peace, the model for which was provided by the natural sciences. Victory was around the corner. Light was seen at the end of the tunnel. Modernization was about to triumph. "We" were all going to share the same world. Oddly enough, "the" world in the singular never appeared more global, total and in the process of completion, than just before the period when the word "globalization" started ringing in our ears.

Another paradox? No, for when globalization is

spoken of nowadays, it is as a fatal danger, a crushing
necessity, a tragedy, a passionate commitment, or as a
challenge to be taken up. In their positive as much as
in their negative renderings, the global or the worldwide are spoken of as a war-like uprising, as a front
or a battle which could be lost. Going global or
worldwide has become a serious problem to be
solved, and is no longer the obvious solution to all
conflicts as it was before, during the times of
modernization. Even the French, despite their fond-
ness for republican universality, rally "against globalization" and start noisily demanding the right to
maintain their "cultural exception"—something that
would have been inconceivable even ten years ago!
They worship a farmer, José Bové, who brings to
Berkeley a smelly Roquefort in order to stop the
American imperialistic grab on food production! For
the first time, the global is becoming visibly and
publicly what is at stake in a merciless war—and no
longer the invisible unity to which everybody surrep-
titiously resorted. Today, in Seattle or Porto Alegre,
barricades go up against globalization and its perils:
who in the past would have been mad enough to put
up barricades against universality? Against nature?

Things look just as bad on the side of multiplicity.
While globalization is causing problems for unity,
fragmentation is now beginning to make tolerance
look equally problematic, if not positively dangerous.
Has anyone sufficiently remarked upon the oddness

of complaining simultaneously about fragmentation, which allegedly prevents any common world, and about globalization, which is blamed for unifying too rapidly and without negotiation? Because, after all, we ought to be rejoicing: if globalization is dangerous, then long live the fragmentation that shatters its hegemony; but if supposedly post-modern fragmentation is so terrifying, should we not be welcoming globalization with open arms, as something which at last provides unity and common sense? In complaining so unfairly against both globalization and fragmentation, we identify precisely the deep transformation that took us out of modernism and the convenient solution it offered to the problems of unity and multiplicity. Fragmentation shatters mononaturalism; globalization destroys multiculturalism. On both sides, whether the aim is to create multiplicity or unity, opponents, fronts and violent contradictions are finally starting to appear. It is possible to measure the staggering speed of transformation with this tell tale sign: the word "global" no longer sounds at all like "natural," and "fragmented" no longer sounds like "culturally respectable." We have seen the last of tolerance, as Isabelle Stengers provocatively said, along with the hypocritical respect of comparative anthropology, and smug assertions about humanity, human rights and the fact that we are all similar inhabitants of the same world. There is now a war of the worlds. Peace, the hypocritical peace of modernity, is well and truly over.

"Qui vis pacem...declare war"

To put things in a more positive and less bellicose way, one might say that we have moved, within the past few years, from a situation of total war led by absolute pacifists, to a situation of open warfare which offers genuine prospects for peace.

The modernists were never really at war since they did not recognize the existence of possible conflicts, except in the realm of superficial representations, which themselves did not really involve the world of nature as it was deciphered by reason. Is it not astounding that the modernists managed to wage war all over the planet without ever coming into conflict with anyone, without ever declaring war? Quite the contrary! All they did was to spread, by force of arms, profound peace, indisputable civilization, uninterrupted progress. They had no adversaries or enemies in the proper sense—just bad pupils. Yes, their wars, their conquests, were educational! Even their massacres were purely pedagogical! We should re-read Captain Cook or Jules Verne: there were fights everywhere and all the time, but always for the good of the people. "That should teach them a lesson…"

Carl Schmitt contends that only where there is no common mediator to whom both sides can turn for arbitration, is there an enemy against whom one could declare war. If this is true, then one can indeed say that that the modernist civilizers never had enemies and modern history has never really witnessed a proper war. Even when fighting fiercely, they always deferred to the authority of an indisputable arbiter, of a mediator far above all possible forms of conflict: Nature and its laws, Science and its unified matters of fact, Reason and its way to reach agreement. When one benefits from a mandate given by a mediator who oversees the conflict, one is no longer running a war but simply carrying out police operations, Schmitt says. Sent to work by the "call of nature" the modernists thus simply policed the world and could say with pride that they had never been at war with anybody.

As a result, of course, they cannot even begin to understand the demands of peace, the writing down of war aims, the necessities of diplomacy, the uncertainties involved in negotiation. "What negotiation? What diplomacy? Which war aims? What peace talks? There is no war! We are just tidying things up, that's all. We are expressing the reality of the order that has always been there, but which collective representations had somewhat obscured." The only wars the modernists ever waged were Wilsonian wars, nature having always given them a mandate more imperative than those of the League of Nations...

It is clear that such latent wars, which never even recognized the enemy's status as an enemy, which considered themselves to be no more than simple police operations undertaken in the name of an indisputable mediator, became as unpacifiable as they were open ended. How could they come to a close if they had never started? How could peace talks be undertaken if war was never declared? Contact need not be established between the two sides of an unbridgeable gulf, since there is no such gulf, only a pre-existing common world whose necessary laws some irrational minds refuse to recognize. Who could negotiate, since the conflict did not involve two sides—and, in any case, there wasn't really a conflict, not a real conflict, not a conflict about reality, only a misunderstanding about symbolic

representations, which themselves might easily co-
exist, on condition of no longer claiming to grasp
reality for good. In the march of civilization, the
Whites have only met the specter of the irrational
and the archaic. They were never faced with
enemies, so how could they ever think about peace?

And yet peace is at stake here, peace is what we
should be longing for. Who could pursue other
goals? Who could delight in being forever at war?
What sort of intellectual would I be if I kept
condoning such bellicose talks? But the question is
how to reach peace.

Of course, the solution cannot be to abandon the
task of composing the common world and take
refuge behind the blinkers and behind the bunkers of
one's own culture, as Samuel Huntington advises us
to do. This would mean believing once again in the
existence of culture and forgetting the task of
creating a common world—not to mention the
horrendous difficulty of partitioning the planet into
homogeneous "civilizations." The whole of Western
history would have been in vain, if we now stoop so
low as to abandon, for good, the promised land of
universality. How could we, the descendants of
centuries of servants of reason, look in the eyes of
our forefathers and tell them without feeling
ashamed that we have given up the worthy goal of
living in one single, common world? It is not this

final goal that is to blame, but only the strange idea that it could be reached without being at war with real enemies. In contrast to the history that sought to modernize, the West has to admit to the existence of war in order to make peace: to accept that it has had enemies, to take seriously the diversity of worlds, to refuse to accept mere tolerance, and to resume the construction of both the local and the global. And it is true that, for this operation to begin, the West will have to go through the most painful period of mourning a unity lost. The common world we took for granted must instead be progressively composed, it is not already constituted. The common world is not behind us and ready made, like nature, but ahead of us, an immense task which we will need to accomplish one step at a time. It is not above us, like the arbiter who mediates conflicts, it is what is at stake in these conflicts, what could become the subject of compromise—should negotiation take place. The common world is now up for grabs.

This brutal transformation may admittedly give Westerners cause for despair: they used to live in peace, they are now at war. They had no enemies; they liked everybody; taking themselves to be by birth global citizens, ready to accept all other cultures no matter how extravagant their diversities. ("Why do other people hate us so much?" ask the post-911 Americans, "when we are so sincere, so plain-spoken, so well-meaning, so good-natured?")

Suddenly, a few years later, here they are, forced to fight again like the others (who meanwhile have ceased to be "others" in the older, modern sense) to define what "global" might really mean, to decide what meaning to give to "multiplicity." They had an infallible solution, they were convinced of the unity of nature and the diversity of cultures, and suddenly they have to start all over again. And yet they have nothing to be despondent about. Their goals remain the same; only the means are different—and the timing. What they thought was a done deal is just beginning anew. Negotiating the sovereignty of Jerusalem might seem like the most difficult of diplomatic quandaries, but what about negotiating the status and the sovereignty of nature, the final arbiter of all conflicts?

Whatever follows modernism at least has the advantage of being clearer. There is no doubt that the war of the worlds is taking place; unity and multiplicity cannot be achieved unless they are progressively pieced together by delicate negotiations. Nobody can constitute the unity of the world for anybody else, as used to be the case (in the times of modernism and later post-modernism), that is, by generously offering to let the others in, on condition that they leave at the door all that is dear to them: their gods, their souls, their objects, their times and their spaces, in short, their ontology. Metaphysics no longer comes after physics but now precedes it as well, and

attempts must be made to develop a protophysics—
an indescribable horror for the modernizing peoples,
but the only hope for those fighting against both
globalization and fragmentation at the same time.
Compared to the light shiver that cultural relativism
might have provoked, this mess, this pandemonium
can only evoke at first repulsion and dismay. It was
precisely to steer clear of all of this horror that
modernism was invented somewhere in the seventeenth century. It was in order to avoid having to put
up with so many worlds, so many contradictory
ontologies and so many conflicting metaphysics, that
they were wisely set up as (in)different entities on the
background of an indisputable (and, alas, meaning-
less) nature full of matters of fact. But nothing
proves that this "bifurcation of nature," as A. N.
Whitehead calls this catastrophic solution, is the
final state of history.

A complete metamorphosis is now required of the
former modernizers: let them look again, right in the
face of this Gorgon they had tried to hide from.
However strange it might seem at first sight, the
modernists, the Westerners, the Whites (whatever
nickname one might wish to give them) will have to
act as if they are once again making contact with the
others for the first time, as if history has given them
an incredible second chance and they were back in
the seventeenth, eighteenth, nineteenth, or twentieth
centuries and are allowed, in the twenty-first, to

introduce themselves properly, they who had intro-
duced themselves so badly in previous centuries
through the most ruthless imperialism. Let them
finally agree that they have enemies, so that they can
make offers of peace.

To arrive unannounced among other peoples and put
everything to fire and the sword with the aim of
pacifying them in the name of a fundamental and
already-constituted peace, is not the same thing, the
same mission, with the same tension, as appearing,
perhaps with the same violence, the same fire and
the same swords, and fighting on the battlefield to
decide which common world should be progressively
pieced together. It is not a matter of replacing intol-
erant conquistadors with specialists of inter-cultural
dialogue. Who ever mentioned dialogue? Who asked
for tolerance? No, conquerors should rather be
replaced by enemies capable of recognizing that
those facing them are enemies also and not irrational
beings, that the outcome of the battle is uncertain,
and that, consequently, it may be necessary to negotiate, and in earnest. While the inter-cultural
dialogue implies that ninety per cent of the common
world is already common and that there is a
universal referee waiting for the parties to settle their
petty disputes, the negotiation we should be
prepared for includes the ninety per cent—God,
Nature and souls included—and there is no arbiter.
The modernists knew on good authority that the

battle was won in advance, since there was no real battle, no battle for reality, only the inevitable march of progress—even if the inexplicable resurgence of archaism (and how indeed could they have explained it?) and the incomprehensible rise of irrationality (and how could they have understood it?) often gave them cause to despair the slow pace of civilization.

Modernism distinguishes itself from its successor— what should it be called? "Second modernity"? "Non-modernity"?— in this one small respect: from now on the battle is about the making of the common world and the outcome is uncertain. That's all. And that's enough to change everything. All those who put up barricades against globalization, all those who fight against fragmentation and disinte-gration, understand the implications of a war which they are at risk of losing.

Two little expressions illustrate this transition, which is as swift as it is imperceptible. The sudden appear-ance, all over the West, of the motif of "risk," intro-duced so efficiently by Ulrich Beck, by no means signifies that life has become more dangerous; it indi-cates rather that everyone has once again, in their day-to-day life, the impression that things could go wrong. For instance, the sky, this very sky my Gallic ancestors feared was about to fall on their heads, could once again fall on our heads and those of our children in the form of radical climate changes.

Back to square one. The first contacts are made, all over again. What? Does this mean we now have to act with care and precaution, like the others, the cowards, the pre-modernists whom the civilizers tried to replace in the risk-free running of the planet? Yes, exactly, and in any case there is today no theme more widespread in Western societies than the principle of precaution, which has of course nothing to do with suspending action, but simply marks the return of anxious and vigilant procedures in the areas connected with science and technology, which were, up until now, characterized by absolute certainty. "Globalization," "disintegration," "risk," "precaution": here are a few of the popular, media-friendly, often despised words which instead point to the world's tremendous sea change, to the ebbing tide of modernism.

What sort of unity? Jus naturalism or constructivism?

Despite the feeling of horror that this change in circumstances might at first provoke in them and in others, what advantages nevertheless arise for the ci-devant modernists! With the opportunity of introducing themselves properly this time, of fighting, of risking loss, comes also the possibility of winning! And for good this time. There is indeed no reason to think that, in piecing together the common world of the future, the Westerners will find themselves at a disadvantage.

On the condition that they don't move, in the mean-
time, from civilizing and modernizing arrogance to
self-flagellation and penitence. The desperate guilt
trip for past crimes committed will get them
nowhere, and neither will it win them forgiveness.
Again, dialogue is not the issue, and neither is tolerance, guilt, nor pardon. What is at stake here is war,
negotiation, diplomacy and the construction of
peace. To castigate oneself, to carry on one's shoul-
ders the white man's crushing burden is nothing
other than continuing to always define by one's self
and in the name of all, without the others having
delegated anything, the impossible task of defining
the common world. Just as no one had asked the
modernists to take themselves for universal pacifiers,
no one asks them today to take themselves for
universal culprits. Only one thing is asked of them
now: that they cease to consider universality as their
own already established territory, and that they
finally agree to negotiate for it after the battle has
taken place. It's just required of them that they
finally become worthy of the prodigious initiative
they once took—no matter if it was due to God, to
Gold or to Science—to come into contact with
others by violence, greed, commerce, conquest,
evangelization, knowledge, management and admin-
istration. No one is even asking them to abandon
their search for universality, since in any case all
peoples now find themselves involved in this other
world war, this fundamental metaphysical war about

the construction of the common space. Now that the task is at hand, it is no longer the time to dress up in a hair shirt and scratch at one's scabs like Job on his dung heap.

Westerners, get up on your feet! It's up to you now to fight for your place in the sun! You perhaps no longer benefit from the absolute winning formula, the martingale which used to ensure your success at every draw, but there is no reason either why you should now always lose. After all, reason is not so weak that it can never win. It has just been a little too long since it had a chance to fight, for lack of real enemies acknowledged as such…Reason has become self-satisfied and complacent, it has got used to the Capuan luxury of naturalism and to its easy complicities. Screaming "relativism!" whenever one is faced with trouble is not enough to keep oneself in good marching order, ready for the extension— yes, the extension—of rationality.

The sticky point is that to the short-term reason of the rationalists, one should add the long-term reason of the diplomat. To be sure diplomats are often hated as potential traitors ready for seedy backroom compromises, but they have the great advantage of getting to work after the balance of forces has become visible on the ground, not before as in the case of police operations. Diplomats know that there exists no superior referee, no arbiter able to declare that the other party is simply irrational and should be disciplined. If a solution is to be found, it is there, among them, with them here and now and nowhere else. Whereas rationalists would not know how to assemble peace talks, as they will not give seats to those they call "archaic" and "irrational," diplomats might know how to organize a parley among declared enemies who, in the sense of Carl Schmitt, may become allies after the peace negotiations have ended. The great quality of diplomats is that they don't know for sure what are the exact and final goals—not only of their adversaries but also of their own people. It is the only leeway they possess, the tiny margin of the negotiations played out in closed rooms. The parties to the conflicts may, after all, be willing to alter slightly what they were fighting for. If you oppose rationalist modernizers to archaic and backward opponents, there is no war, to be sure, but there is no possible peace either. Negotiation cannot even start. Reason recognizes no enemy. But the outcome might be entirely different if you pit proponents of different common worlds one against the other. Because then diplomats could begin to realize that there are different ways to achieve the goals of the parties at war, including their own. Nothing proves in advance that modernizers might not be willing to modify the ways to achieve their cherished goals if they were shown that the cult of nature makes it impossible to reach them.

To formulate their peace offers, to present themselves more politely than before, to introduce the
talks in a less counter-productive way, the former
modernists, for instance, could introduce a distinc-
tion between jus naturalism and constructivism. The
term "natural law" is predominantly used in legal
theory, but it is also perfectly suited to define the
whole of the modernist solution, on condition that
the notion of "rule" be extended to include physical
laws: there exists out there a nature whose necessary
laws make it possible to judge by contrast the diversity of cultural idiosyncrasies. However, jus naturalism is not the modernists' only tradition: they
possess another, almost contradictory, tradition that
is much richer and that we can call constructivist.
Facts, as their etymology indicates, are fabricated,
and so are fetishes, gods, values, works of art, political arenas, landscapes and nations.

At first glance though, the notion of construction
does not seem very compelling, since it suffers from
one of modernism's major faults: it is usually associ-
ated with social construction and with the vocabu-
lary of criticism. When we say that nature is
"constructed," that God must be "produced," that
the person must be "fabricated," it is immediately
assumed we are attacking, undermining, criticizing
their supposed solidity. "So," one could object,
outraged, "neither nature, nor the divinities, nor
persons 'really' exist; they are 'pure' fabrications,

'simple' social constructions? How could we not lose in those new parleys if we were presenting only to the others our constructivist profile?" And yet, we might suggest that the former modernists are the only ones to make this opposition: for the others (the former "others"), construction rhymes with production, authentication and qualification. More exactly, it is the very notion of jus naturalism that forces the opposition with "artificial," "human," "subjective," "fabricated." After all, even the very word "fact" designates what is fabricated and what is real and beyond fabrication after the fabrication has taken place. Constructivism, if we understand it in this new (very old) positive sense, would have no opposite.

While the concept of nature implies antonyms, for instance culture, the notion of construction could serve as a lingua franca for beginning to understand each other. From both sides of the table (if indeed it is a table) one would then hear: "At least we can be sure of one thing: that your gods as much as ours, your worlds as much as ours, your sciences as much as ours, your selves as much as ours, are constructed." The relevant question for the diplomats would no longer be, "Is it or isn't it constructed?" but rather: "How do you manufacture them?" And, above all, "How do you verify that they are well constructed?" Here is where negotiations could begin: with the question of the right ways to build.

This is where the mourning should take place, *le travail du deuil*, because this result leaves Westerners without what they believed was their highest virtue. They must face their loss—the loss of the possibility of reaching assent by an appeal to external nature. Exactly the opposite is the case: by definition, an agreement about nature cannot be reached, because the notion of "nature" itself has been made, as we have seen, to prevent a progressive agreement about the slow composition of the common world. With nature, unity is always the one thing that is no longer at stake, which does not need to be negotiated. Once nature enters the debate, others have only subjective and biased representations of it. If they persist in clinging to those representations, they are simply irrational. On the other hand, if gods, persons, objects and worlds are taken to be "constructed" entities, that is, entities that could fail (and the notion of construction implies nothing else), then here is perhaps a means of opening the peace talks again by rephrasing the war aims of all parties. Such is the event no one could foresee, the major transformation that has been going on for the last decades and that the label postmodernism covers so badly: contrary to modernists' beliefs up to now, nature cannot be generalized, while constructivism, in contrast, may be shared by all—at least it is worth a new diplomatic attempt. You cannot dream any longer of the modern definition of nature extending to the whole planet, but you might be able to go a long way towards the goal of unity by confronting good and bad constructions of worlds.

It is at this turning point in the negotiations that the former modernists could appeal to their own resources, forgotten or hidden by modernism and its pretensions. The modernists felt, by definition, uncomfortable in the borrowed garb of modernization. For indeed, if modernization cannot give an account of others, since it forces them into a far too exaggerated otherness, how could it give an account of Westerners? The Whites have never been modern, either. If it is unfair to portray the peoples who were civilized as irrational or as archaic survivors on their way towards a single world, it is even more unfair to describe the civilizing peoples as rational and modern. This would be a form of inverted exoticism. "Modernism" or "Occidentalism" in this context may be understood in the sense of "Orientalism": it is equivalent to seeing the Europeans or the Americans with the perspective—all tropical palms, secluded harems and painted savages—that they themselves adopt towards other cultures. In other words, as long as the modernists are taken to be what they say they are, one treats them with the same cheap exoticism one finds disgusting in the tourist brochures when applied to other peoples. Peace negotiations are not possible unless both sides give up exoticism and its perverse complacency with the false difference introduced by the one nature-many cultures divide. Likewise, diplomacy cannot begin until we suspend our assumptions about what does or does not count as difference. There are more ways than one to differ—and thus more than one way to agree—in the end.

In this respect, the former modernists are perhaps better off than they believe, and will be able to supply more answers to questions relating to proper methods of construction than they thought, in the days when they paraded about, dressed up as a civilizing people. But to do that they have to sort out their heritage: they should be proud of its universalistic goals, but not of its of its first "naturalist" attempts to realize them. Let us try to bring them back to the negotiating table, but this time let them approach politely, showing the others their constructivist face instead of their naturalizing gaze. Rather than take the defining elements of the modernist constitution off the table (Science, Nature, God, the Individual, Economics and Politics) as points beyond any discussion or concession, what if they accepted these as matters to be resolved in a negotiation involving all the parties to the composition of the common world?

Take the example of research. It is one thing to present oneself to the world under the cover of universal Science, and quite another to present oneself as producer and manufacturer of local and risk-laden sciences—with a small "s." In the first case, the recipients of such an offer only have the option of withdrawing into the irrational, or of humbly changing sides and submitting to the modernists' pedagogy. The second case is much more uncertain: the sciences make suggestions or "propositions" that lengthen the list of beings with which the common world must be pieced together, but still more propositions may be made by others, making this list even longer and complicating yet further the learned confusion. A universal Science cannot be negotiated and thus it cannot be universalized for good, but sciences that aspire to incremental or emergent universalization can.

Independent, asocial matters of fact cannot bring about agreement, but hairy, entangled states of affairs may, in the end. And the modernists already produce both at the same time: they have put forth an image of Science as a political project of unification without negotiation; but, meanwhile, they also produce multiple, attractive and complex sciences which may participate in multiple projects of unification or localization, depending on the outcome of the conflicts. The diplomatic issue has shifted: can the modernists be saved from themselves, so that they may share the sciences with others and leave Science aside—this Science that they believed up to now to be non-negotiable, like the status of

Jerusalem, the thrice-holy city? Can the diplomats, without being seen as traitors, offer to retain the power of the sciences and to let Science go so that universality could eventually be better composed?

Take the case of religion, which, even more than Science, has to do with earlier, premature modernist projects to unify the planet. Can a positive constructivism be applied in this instance? Might not the nearly fanatic attachment to the non-constructed character of the unity of God be largely a response to the unifying role of nature, which the negotiations have agreed to limit? If the latter becomes negotiable, why not the former too? Do we mandate the diplomats to dare to say, during the peace negotiations, for instance, of the God of Abraham, Isaac and Jacob, that he is well or badly constructed? Do we allow them to point to the objects, the rituals, prayers and the manufacturing kits that would allow it to be compared with the ways of producing other kinds of divinities? How could such an offer not be revolting, scandalous, blasphemous? Would it not amount to a reversion to the horrible archaism against which the great religions of the Book took their stand? And yet, the comparison with nature is enlightening. If "nature" was a political concept that tried to unify too quickly and without piece-by-piece composition of the common world, could not the same be said of the unity of God? Just as sciences differ profoundly from Science, might not the diplomat discover in religious practices the tell tale signs of constructivism? What do we know about the religions of the former modernists? The discourse of fabrication, invention and deception has, until now, mostly been used for critical denunciation. Why not use it positively, and re-formulate, in the company of the others, the question of the right ways of constructing good divinities? Would we not have here, instead of a hypothetical "interreligious dialogue," a more fruitful and even technical exchange of procedures? The all powerful already existing absolute God sends his devout to holy war, but what about the relative God which might be unified in the slowly constructed future?

Take the case of the manufacture of persons. It is one thing to claim to have discovered the free and rights-bearing individual by asserting that it must be generalized to the whole world; it is quite another to add to the astounding history of the elaboration of human masks, the "personae," the strange composition of the modern self. In the first case the starting point is the indisputable fact that there are individuals and that they are all free and human; in the second case, we bring to the negotiating table a character that is particularly bound, charged up, weighted down by this peculiar history: the Western Individual. The modernist subject does not enter the discussion to put things in order, nor does it offer the one and only face concealed beneath all the variations: rather, it is another kind of visage to add to the series—and the least one can say in its favor is that this figure does not stand out as particularly unusual in the great procession of the masks proposed by the "others." If in the first case, modern psychology constitutes the indisputable base of all humanity, in the other the components of the Western psyche appear so local, so provincial, so costly and elaborate that they surely cannot be generalized instantly, at a single stroke. Here again, nothing can speed up the negotiation: most other parties to the conflict do not recognize that there are humans, subjects, individuals or rights-bearers; instead of exploring the free-floating individual they have multiplied the attachments—gods, fetishes lineages, ancestors—that produce possible subjectivities; for them the Western individual is a monster that should be fiercely resisted. But again, if we authorize our diplomats to present our types of subjectivities and all of the complex institutions and belonging that make it seem free-floating, then the negotiations might resume in earnest. After all, modernist subjects too are possessed by what Tobie Nathan calls their "owners," their "proprietors," the divinities that make them hold together and that do not reside in the inner sanctum of private subjectivity. Once this price has been paid, is it not possible to think that the rights-bearing human, the free individual might win in the end—but this time for good?

Economics too has naturalistic and constructivist faces. It is one thing to present the market forces as the natural bedrock of all humanity since the beginning of time, as the fundamental logic to which everyone should submit without discussion in order to enjoy the benefits of wealth and freedom; it is quite another to present market organizations as a rare, local, fragile set of mechanisms to explore the many attachments of people and goods and to calculate, through risky and disputable accounts, what they are worth and how they should be distributed. The first presentation is not negotiable and to oppose it is tantamount to archaism, backwardness, localism and irrationality. The second deploys a rather large arena for legitimate dissent about how to calculate, what to take into account, how to modify market organization. Is it really rational to believe in the inevitable extension of *Homo economicus* to the whole planet? Strangely enough, this most obviously contingent Western elaboration is also the one that Westerners have tried to naturalize most! Is it really asking too much of our diplomats that they recognize the legitimacy of dissent in matters of economics? The question is not simply to add some human values to the harsh reality of the "dismal science," but to see how complex is the entanglement we call a "market," something which is so obviously constructed, so clearly local that it cannot be spread without further ado. What will we really lose in acknowledging the essential negotiability of market organizations?

Finally, take the example of politics. Here again, as always, the former modernists issued two contradictory messages, the first one a war cry (all the while denying that war was taking place): humanity will be democratic or it will not be rightfully constituted. The second message indicates a profound uncertainty about the nature of politics: is it a question of representation, cohesion, solidarity, a common world, liberties, tradition, obedience, rule of law or civility? In the first case, the rest of humanity has no other choice than to prove that it can also be a representative democracy—even if imitation often results in caricature. In the second case, the question of how to define "politics" is re-opened; and the outcome here, as always, is once again uncertain.

Those who want to extend the rule of law and democratic debates to the whole earth should know the price they are asking others to pay in terms of institutions, forms of life, habits, media, courts, values, feelings. If there is one institution that has to be carefully constructed, one which is even more fragile than the ecosystems of a coral reef, it is the practice of democracy. It is one thing to request that everywhere citizens should assemble in democratic agoras; it is another to recognize that for the largest part of humanity and the longest part of history, other types of assemblages have been sought, arrangements in which humans were only tiny participants. Here again should we mandate our diplomats to teach everyone how to behave like a citizen or should we also encourage them to learn, along with their opponents, how to practice the much more difficult but much longer-lasting task of cosmopolitics—meaning, in the terms of Isabelle Stengers, the politics of the cosmos?

Whether in matters of science, religion, psychology, economics or politics, the former modernists clearly have more than one trick up their sleeve. The reason they have appeared so clumsy up to now in making offers of peace is because they did not think there was any war, and then, modernization seemed to them so obvious that it was not open to any compromise. Further, when they started having doubts about modernization and they became postmodern, they became even more clumsy because they replaced arrogance with guilt, but without entering into more negotiations than they had before. It is now time to help them, to bring them tactfully to the negotiating table, making sure they recognize that there is indeed a war of the worlds, and helping them carefully distinguish between what they thought was worth dying for—universality—from what they really care about—the construction of universality. As always, the parties in the conflict do not know exactly what they are fighting for. The task of the diplomats is to help them find out.

And, of course, their offer of mediation, like mine, may fail. ■

Acknowledgments

Translated from the French by Charlotte Bigg. The occasion to write this piece was provided in August 2000 by the meeting "Guerre et paix des cultures" organized by Tobbie Nathan and Isabelle Stengers at Cerisy La Salle. I thank the participants for many helpful comments. It has been revised in December 2001 and again in April 2002 thanks to John Tresch's careful reading. I have also greatly benefited from remarks by Eduardo Viveiros de Castro, Sophie Houdard and Masato Fukushima.

Further Readings

Callon, M., ed. 1998. *The Laws of the Market*. Oxford: Blackwell.

Christin, O. 1997. *La paix de religion. L'autonomisation de la raison politique au 16° siècle*. Paris: Le Seuil.

Descola, P. and G. Palsson, eds. 1996. *Nature and Society. Anthropological Perspectives*. London: Routledge.

Jurdant, B., ed. 1998. *Impostures intellectuelles. Les malentendus de l'affaire Sokal*. Paris: La Découverte.

Latour, B. 1999. *Politiques de la nature. Comment faire entrer les sciences en démocratie*. Paris: La Découverte.

Lévi-Strauss, C. [1952]1987. *Race et histoire*. Paris: Denoël.

Nathan, T. 1994. *L'influence qui guérit*. Paris: Editions Odile Jacob.

Sahlins, M. 1995. *How "Natives" Think: About Captain Cook, for Example*. Chicago: University of Chicago Press.

Stengers, I. 1997. *Cosmopolitiques - Tome 7: 'pour en finir avec la tolérance'*. Paris: La Découverte & Les Empêcheurs de penser en rond.

_____. 1996. *Cosmopolitiques - Tome 1: la guerre des sciences*. Paris: La Découverte & Les Empêcheurs de penser en rond.

Viveiros de Castro, E. 1998. *"Les pronoms cosmologiques et le perspectivisme amérindien"* in E. Alliez (ed.), *Gille Deleuze. Une vie philosophique*. Paris: Les Empêcheurs de penser en rond, pp. 429-462.